D1633212

0136190288

# Writing for Magazines in the UK: how to get paid to write

# Writing for Magazines in the UK:
## the UK:
### how to get paid to write

Ellie Stevenson

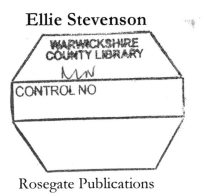

Rosegate Publications

First published in 2015 by Rosegate Publications

ISBN 978-0-9572165-7-0

Cover design by James Allwright

# CONTENTS

# A. Introduction

**What's different about this writer's guide?**
It's short, to the point and it pulls no punches.

If you're a writer – especially if you write for magazines, you don't have time to waste on waffle. You need to get to the point, and fast. You also need to know the facts – and this guide aims to do both for you. If you find that some of the points are repeated – take note – it means these points are particularly crucial.

And now... read on.

# B. Why Consider Writing for Magazines in the First Place?

It's an opportunity to write about what you're interested in, and what you know. Most people know about something: from gardening to woodwork, cooking to childcare. And then there's what you do for a living. The possibilities are endless.

If you're lucky, work smartly and depending on how much time you put in, you may gain some additional income. It's very hard to earn a living writing for magazines. It can be done, but it's very difficult. This guide points you in the right direction.

It's flexible work: which means it's a fit with those who have home-based commitments, like caring for people. You can work it around your other tasks.

Last, but not least, it's a good way to gain experience and put together a writing portfolio. It will help you sharpen specific skills: skills all writers need to have. What are those skills? See below.

**So far, so good. There must be some drawbacks?**

- It's a very competitive field to be in. It's hard to get work
- And the pay's not good: you have to be very self-motivated. It's probably much easier to get a job at your local supermarket
- Specific skills or qualities are required if you're to be effective and sell your work

But, don't lose heart, many of these skills can be learnt or developed, and honed with practice and a willingness to continue.

# C. What Skills and Qualities are Needed?

- The ability to write (both the article itself, and succinct pitches to magazine editors). Some writers are better than others. To some it comes naturally, to others it doesn't. But if it's something you want to achieve, you can always improve and find your own style. To do that, of course, needs practice

- Commitment to working and keeping on going, even when you feel disheartened. This is very much related to:
  - having confidence or the willingness to develop it, and the ability to put your ego aside and not let setbacks get you down
  - you need to be able to focus and work to deadlines, your own and others (warning: keeping to your own is *much* harder)
  - the ability to select from the research available, and summarise effectively. This is a skill that can be learnt or honed, with sufficient practice. It's very important
  - good verbal communication skills: for

interviewing people and (very occasionally) talking to editors

- the need to be decisive, on a regular basis: choosing what you will do and when you will do it
- computer literacy: editors will need typed pieces and email is the usual contact method
- strong organisational skills for making it happen and keeping on top of your various projects

So, assuming you have all of the above, or are willing to develop them, how to begin?

# D. The Practicalities

There are numerous magazines out there, as many as there are people and interests. From sport to hobbies to investment and women's magazines, there is no shortage of potential markets.

## 1. Identify Topics to Write On

Your first task is to identify subjects you want to write on. These are usually ones in which you have knowledge or expertise. And, of course, an interest.

It might be something you do/have done for a living. It might be a hobby, or home-based work, like sewing, or DIY.

Do you have a broad knowledge of this topic?

Writers don't have to be experts in a topic: what you do need is a basic knowledge, a good grounding, which can then be topped up with research or interviews. You can update yourself or talk to someone about a specialist aspect, but won't have time to start from scratch.

Draw up a list of topics or subjects.

## 2. Identify Markets covering your Topics

The next stage is to find suitable markets, i.e. magazines, which cover these topics.

- Visit shops and libraries and browse their shelves, looking at the magazines and getting an idea of their content. Make a note of possible magazines

- Study the *Writers' & Artists' Yearbook* (UK). Your local library may have a copy

- Search Google for magazines: put in terms which define your topic, e.g. 'steam railways magazine' 'world war history magazine' and see what comes up

- Talk to your contacts: so for example, if you work in finance and think you could write on how to complete a tax return, talk to your colleagues about magazines or publications they read which might cover that area. Professional journals are another useful market to try, depending on the topic, as are in-house magazines

- You can also subscribe to Freelance Market News (www.freelancemarketnews.com): this is a newsletter giving useful information on markets for writing

- Browse or subscribe to *Writers' Forum* (www.writers-forum.com) or *Writing Magazine* (www.writers-online.co.uk/Writing-Magazine): these are generic writing magazines but they include current market information

Be open to possibilities but do be selective and discriminating: ask yourself whether you want this magazine on your portfolio?

Having done the above, you should now have a provisional list of possible markets (magazines).

# 3. Confirm your Chosen Markets accept Articles from Freelancers

Some magazines have their own in-house writers or freelance team and will not accept submissions from other writers.

You should always pitch for a commission before you write an article – more about that below – but for now you just need to confirm that they accept articles from freelance writers, before you do any more research on the magazine.

This information is most easily obtained from the *Writers' & Artists' Yearbook*. Look up the section: Magazines UK and Ireland and identify magazines of interest. Under each title will be information about content, what they will consider accepting, length required and sometimes payment. (For those wanting American markets, there is another publication, *Writer's Market*).

## 4. Getting to Know your Markets

Once you've identified several magazines you might like to write for, and which accept freelance submissions, you need to become familiar with them.

You should have a list which is always growing,

but pick out two to three magazines to work on, to begin with.

**Study these in more depth.** This needn't cost a lot of money. Apart from browsing through them in shops, most magazines will have an online presence (website) and some will send you a free back issue if you ask them and explain why you want one.

**Read their style guidelines:** these may be on their website, or if not, you can email the magazine and ask them to send you a copy (not all magazines have style guidelines but it is worth asking).

## Why do I have to do this?

Scanning the magazine/website will give you a better idea of the type of topic covered *and* the way it is handled. Does the magazine take a serious or a more light-hearted approach. Is the style educational or conversational?

Style guidelines will generally give you information like how many words are required, etc, but style is also about approach: the length of paragraphs, formal or informal discussion, etc.

You also need to ask yourself who the readers are: amateur gardeners, students, young people with an interest in sport, etc. What kind of income/lifestyle might they have?

All these things affect the way you write your article, and the style guide will give you tips on these, as will articles in the same magazine by other writers.

Successful magazine writing is about fit for purpose – will the content of your article fit with the magazine's portfolio or brand? If it doesn't, it won't be accepted, however well-written it might be.

## 5. Approaching Magazines

### So I just write the article and send it off then?

Definitely not. You should always pitch for a commission to write an article, not just write it. This means approaching the magazine with a proposal BEFORE you start to write.

The only situation in which you might just write a piece and send it off could be when you are new to the business and need the experience. But even so, this is not advisable, as time is money and you will have spent time and effort researching and writing something which a magazine might not want.

## The professional way is to pitch for the work first.

## How do I approach the magazine?

Look under the heading for that particular magazine in the *Writers' & Artists' Yearbook* (UK) or on the magazine itself (usually at the front or back) or on the magazine website. This will give information relevant to that particular publication.

When, for example, it says in the *Writers' & Artists' Yearbook* something like 'no unsolicited material' this means a query (as advised above) is essential.

## Tips for Sending a Query Email (pitch)

Address your email to a **named person as shown in the magazine or on their website** – you may have to ring up the magazine and ask who this is, but DON'T attempt to pitch by phone, unless you already have a working relationship with the editor in question. Editors are busy and don't welcome such calls.

Keep your pitch short and to the point.

## What should my query email contain?

- A short paragraph outlining the proposed article or feature
- A further two lines, saying what it will contain and why it's relevant
- Two more lines outlining your relevant experience

## Sample Email

Dear Ms Jones

I'm writing to propose an article on the benefits of holidaying in Tasmania, highlighting the upcoming film festival and ten-year celebrations.

The piece will discuss some of the most exotic places to stay and showcase the main tourist attractions illustrating this with anecdotal comments/quotes from recent visitors.

I am a freelance writer and former travel agent with over fifteen years' experience in travel and tourism.

I look forward to hearing from you.

With kind regards [or best wishes]

John Smith

**DON'T send more than one query (i.e. one suggested topic) to any one editor at one time.**

An editor may refuse your proposal but may ask for an alternative (if, for example, she has a piece on that in the pipeline already). Be prepared; have other ideas you can pitch to the editor straight away, **if she asks**, rather than lose the opportunity.

**Does it matter how long in advance I pitch for a commission?**

Very much so. Magazines (like many other organisations) are always planning ahead so you should be too. For some magazines and some content there is no time element, e.g. an article on how to get a job may fit into the magazine at any time of year, but if you are writing about the ideal summer holiday then timescale is important.

You should pitch four months ahead for weekly magazines and six months ahead for monthly magazines. You don't want someone else to get there first!

## Photographs

If you have photographs to support the article, say so, that's a big plus.

**DON'T** send the photographs with the query email.

**DO** make sure that you have the rights to any photographs you may wish to send, so, for example, you took them yourself.

**DO** make sure (even if you did take the photos) that any people in them have given their permission for the photos to be used.

## What are my chances of success, once I've sent my query email?

The reality is, not very high, but you will increase your chances significantly by studying the magazine, its style and its recent content before pitching.

## Even if your pitch is good, you might not be

**successful because:**

- Something has just been published on that topic (one of the reasons why it's important to research the magazine properly)
- They have something lined up on that theme already
- A competing magazine is running a similar topic at the same time
- Your idea doesn't fit with what the editor wants **at that time**

In most cases, you'll probably only hear from the editor if he wants to commission the piece or is interested in commissioning something else. A lack of response (if the editor isn't interested) is quite common.

If you don't hear, it's alright to chase pitches after about two weeks, but **only by email.**

You can increase your chances of success when pitching by making sure your proposal is a good fit for the magazine's content *and* hasn't been covered recently.

Also, start small. It's important to choose

magazines you want to write for, but don't aim for ones with massive circulations on your very first week!

Should you get any feedback from the editor (you usually won't), take note of the feedback, but remember it may only apply to that magazine.

## What if I don't succeed with my pitch?

If you hear nothing, or get a refusal, don't take it personally. This is a very competitive field. Be businesslike and move on to the next pitch.

## How many pitches should I send per week?

That depends on your reason for writing.

If this is just a spare-time activity, you can send out pitches whenever you want to or have the material.

But if you are aiming to make this a business, or a significant self-employment activity, you need to send out at least 10 per week, most likely more.

Imagine you receive £100 for a commission, and only one in ten of your pitches is successful (which is quite possible), then your earnings per month would be around £400 before tax; a nice additional income but nowhere near self-supporting. You need to be clear about what you want to achieve from the work and set your targets accordingly.

**Develop an action plan:** the pitches you want to send and when, and the editors you want to send them to and just keep going. Although, **don't** obviously, inundate one particular editor with lots of pitches, even one after the other. This will only annoy people.

## What happens if my pitch is successful and the editor is interested?

Agree with the editor:

a) When the article is needed by
b) Any other requirements the editor may have
c) Payment (be realistic; writing isn't very well paid, particularly in the current climate)
d) If you're providing photos, you need to clarify
   - if there will be additional payment for these and
   - in what format they are to be supplied
e) What rights you are selling, e.g. First British Serial Rights. First British Serial Rights means that the magazine gets to use it before anyone

else, in the UK. If, for example, these are the rights you've agreed, you can then sell the same or a similar piece elsewhere, e.g. abroad, ideally after some time has elapsed.

Increasingly, when you sell rights, this can include the electronic rights (i.e. the magazine will put the article online). You should clarify whether this is so, in advance.

## 6. Writing the Article

**Before you start writing, remember:**

- You must be computer literate – editors will expect a document in Word or similar
- To study the magazines guidelines (if there are any) and previous articles for tips on style and presentation – **match your style to the magazine's style** (chatty, formal, short and snappy, more descriptive, long paragraphs, short paragraphs, etc)
- Equally, your content should fit with the magazine's content – you should already be aware of this, from when you did your pitch
- Articles should be well written and proofread before submission – editors get surprisingly

large numbers of submissions with poor grammar and spelling
* Decide how much time to spend on the article (research and the writing) **before** you write it

## How do I know how much time to spend?

If this is a business, rather than a hobby, you need to be able to produce high-quality articles **quickly**. That takes practice, but get into good habits from the very beginning.

Do enough research, but no more than you need. It is very easy to spend too much time researching.

Based on the payment you will receive or are prepared to accept, work out **before you start** how much time (writing and research) to spend on the piece. **Time is money.**

So, for example, if you are to be offered £150 for the piece and you think you could work for £15 per hour (before tax) then you have 10 hours to research and write the piece. If the piece is 1,000 words then you may feel you need 3 hours to write it, 1-2 hours for editing and proofing, which leaves 5 hours for research and phone calls to get quotes.

Obviously the figures and times are adjustable to suit your own abilities/requirements/earnings but get into the habit of producing work to the time you set yourself. It's a good discipline and even if you think you can spare the extra time now, if in the future you get busy, that discipline will make you more effective and your work more profitable.

Don't be too concerned about working for small amounts in the beginning as relevant writing experience will be valuable for your portfolio, but your time is valuable too, so whatever limits you set yourself, stick to them.

Managing one's own time, and not doing additional effectively unpaid work is one of the hardest disciplines freelance writers have to learn.

## Interviewing

If you're writing a feature article (and sometimes if you're not) you will want quotes to back up your piece. Two quotes (from two different people) per article are usually enough. Quotes add flavour and interest to a piece; interviewing people (whether or not you quote them) is a useful way to get additional specialist information that you've been unable to discover through your research. Often, for an article, a broad understanding is sufficient, but talking to specialists in that area can add additional insight.

Like setting limits and keeping to them, interviewing people, probably mostly by phone, is one of the harder aspects of writing articles in the beginning. You may have to identify sources of experts (e.g. by contacting a company or organisation), then pick up the phone and ask to talk to them, explaining why and how the material will be used. This can be scary in the beginning, especially as some people will refuse.

If so, don't be daunted, try someone else.

Interviewing people is a topic in itself but key things to remember are:

- Many people will be happy to talk to you, but if the person you approach isn't, don't be dismayed, just say thank you and try someone else
- If you wish to record the interview, you MUST ask the interviewee's permission beforehand
- Never quote someone without their permission and make sure they know in

advance what you are going to say
- If you quote someone, it's good manners to email the quote to them beforehand, for them to approve

## 7. I've written my piece and I've no more work. What Now?

A professional writer always has irons in the fire. If you've completed all your pieces of work there is always something else you can do.

- Pitch for more commissions
- Chase any outstanding pitches – but only if you've left them **at least two weeks**
- Continue your investigation into suitable subjects to write about, and markets
- Keep up to date with the content of magazines you already know about (very important)
- Keep a list of ideas for articles and keep adding to it
- Keep a list of magazines you want to write for and keep adding to it
- Prepare a calendar of dates and look at the possibility for time-focused articles, e.g. Christmas, Easter, anniversaries. There are

websites available which connect the date to an event or theme. Use these to identify topics which connect with a date. Remember the rule about pitching sufficiently far in advance: this is particularly pertinent when you have a time-based deadline

Such activity, as well as increasing your chances of success, will maintain your morale during the inevitable quiet periods or after a rejection.

# 8. Writing and Tax

If you earn money from your writing you will need to declare this to the Inland Revenue. To find out more about working for yourself, registering for self-assessment and the different types of business model, from sole traders to partnerships, visit the Inland Revenue website at:

**www.gov.uk/working-for-yourself**

You can also find more information here:

**www.gov.uk/self-employed-records**

Alternatively, you can contact them by phone

on **0300 200 3310.**

It's important that you investigate tax and national insurance matters as soon as possible. Don't delay in completing the relevant paperwork!

# 9. Is There More I can Do?

The above are all things you should be doing, in between commissions. But on a longer term basis there are other things you can do, to raise your profile and increase your success.

Sell similar material to the content you've researched to a different market. The secret here is creativity. It's not just about having the knowledge, but applying it appropriately, to different markets.

So, for example:

Change the angle: an article on changes in train travel (travel or history magazine) could be adapted to be about the psychology of train travel (a women's magazine).

Broaden your topic for a popular, non-specialist market like a women's magazine, e.g. from the history of reading to why people read or how they read now.

Sell the same content elsewhere, tweaked for that market. US and foreign markets are a typical example. (You can find information about United States magazine markets in *Writer's Market*; www.writersmarket.com) This is quite acceptable providing you haven't sold all your rights to the first magazine. It's also acceptable to do this in the UK (again providing you haven't sold all your rights, just First rights) but it may be harder to find a market and you would be advised to let a period of time go by or tweak the angle.

Ask yourself if there are any personal stories you want to share, e.g. our life in a new country, changing my career from actor to aviator. The tone of such pieces may be more informal, but articles should still have a professional feel and be discreet. Remember to discuss such ideas with anyone else involved in the project.

Don't ignore websites as a potential market but apply the same principles of professionalism as with magazines and make sure they pay for the work. Many websites are more interested in free content. If you write a piece for a magazine, you should check whether it will be going on their website too.

As you become more experienced, you may consider trying to get a column. Regular work from a magazine is a welcome additional source of income and it sometimes allows more flexibility in the content you write. Not easy to get, but worth looking out for: find out which of your chosen magazines has a regular column written by a freelancer.

Embrace technology: things are changing fast in IT – keep up to date with the latest trends and ask yourself how these could help your work.

When you have sufficient output (articles), consider getting a website to showcase it. This needn't be expensive, both WordPress and Google's Blogger offer free, easy to set up, websites. Here you can showcase your work to others by providing a list of articles and contact information. **Don't** post the whole article – just the title, a two line summary (if you wish) and a link to the magazine, **after** it has been published. Always include a short bio, and keep it professional – no cute pictures or casual rant. This is a business website.

If you decide to have a website (and WordPress is easy to set up and use), you **must** keep it up to date. Out of date websites don't inspire confidence in the writer.

Social Media, like Twitter or Facebook, is a great way to promote your brand and your work. But please remember:

- Social media is a public platform – only say things you'd want editors to see. Be professional at all times
- Think about posts from the editor's perspective – would s/he want you to post about this
- The editor will have paid for rights to the article – which means you can mention it but may not be able to share the content

# E. The Publishing Perspective: what would an editor say to me?

It's a difficult climate, publishers are facing increasing challenges with the wealth of websites in existence and the problems of getting their magazines into retail outlets. They often have to tighten their belts.

**To increase your chances of success:**

- Be constantly adding to your lists of magazines and ideas
- Make sure you study each magazine's guidelines: tailor your style and content to theirs
- Focus: send out plenty of well-prepared pitches each week **and keep records of them**
- Be literate (article *and* pitch) – check your spelling or grammar, and if you're uncertain, ask someone else to check your articles for you
- If you're not computer savvy, get some training. Editors expect well-presented, word-

processed documents and correspondence is usually by email

- Magazines are frequently niche markets: a lot of them, especially the smaller ones, struggle to get relevant content, but equally that means they won't pay very much
- Writers have to write for the love of writing – you won't become rich (that's the bad news), although it is possible to make money, **if you're professional, fast and keep going.** Don't be deterred by rejection, be businesslike and move on to the next pitch

*'If it fits with what we do I'm interested'* Alistair Brewin (director, Brewin Books)

## So, writers, what are you waiting for?

If you've enjoyed this writers' guide you might want to read some of Ellie Stevenson's fiction. **See the excerpts in the following pages.**

# F. Shadows of the Lost Child
(Extract from the novel)

## by **Ellie Stevenson**

Rosegate Publications, 2014
ISBN: 978-0-9572165-5-6

### About Shadows of the Lost Child

Would children crying keep you awake?
Especially if the children were dead?

A haunted house, a man with a past and a girl
called Alice who can cross time.

Then Alice meets Tom who lives in the past and
the past and the present begin to collide... with
fatal consequences.

**This is a ghost story, and a tragedy that
happened over a century ago.**

**And a mystery. Can *you* solve it?**
Inspired by the legends of York (UK)

# 1
# Now – Aleph

I've always lived in the shadow of churches. Now, when I see one, I walk the other way.

It was Thursday morning, the beginning of spring. I walked down Narrowboat Lane to the arch, and under the archway onto the street. I saw the house, it was over to the left; it looked quite something. Then I raised my eyes above the windows and saw what was towering high above it. An enormous church. A single word sprang to my lips. Or maybe two.

'Hell,' I said. 'Hell and damnation.'

Not just a church behind the house, but a great big giant, a monster of a thing, all gables and parapets, much more like a cathedral really. My heart sank, for I knew what it meant, another place I'd have to turn down.

'Curdizan Abbey,' said the voice beside me, 'and don't say no to the house just yet. It has some truly *amazing* features.' I shook my head and looked to the right and there was Gemma, from Cloud House Properties. The word *amazing* wasn't strictly accurate. I imagined the house had draughty rooms and uneven floors, and doors that didn't quite fit properly. But, what did I think the woman would say? She was an estate agent after all. Gemma Pearce held out her hand.

'Good to meet you, Mr Jones.'

'Good to meet *you*,' I said, smiling, and grasped her hand which was small and neat. She was blonde, beautiful, tall and thin with china doll features and perfect straight hair. I could feel the benefits of the house already.

We moved a bit closer and she jangled her keys, and a flash of the sun caught the edge of the steel. A sharp strip of light fell down from the sky, splitting the steps up ahead in two. There was light and dark and I knew which side of the steps were mine. I raised my head and there was the abbey, all of a shimmer. It almost felt like some kind of welcome.

'It seems to me it's yours already,' said Gemma coyly, as she pushed on the door, which was old and warped. I followed her in.

*No*, I thought, as we entered the hall, *it's not my house*. But it was, really.

Later that day I was standing inside the estate agent's office. The lovely Gemma had long since gone, leaving me there with somebody different. Exceedingly different. Her eyes were cold and her face disapproving.

'You're *self-employed*?' she said, frowning. 'We'll have to see your accounts, I'm afraid.'

'But I don't have any accounts,' I said. 'I don't earn enough to be VAT registered.' I could feel the palms of my hands sweating. This wasn't going the way I'd hoped.

'Well, what about your tax returns? We do need to see you can cover the rent.'

The way she was making me feel right now, I doubted I could. I said nothing.

'Do you have any other assets? A house, perhaps, or maybe some savings?' I shook my head. *Nothing*, I thought, *that's what I've got.*

Before, I'd lived in my girlfriend's flat, I hadn't needed any assets, not even things like a washing machine. We'd shared possessions, plates and everything. I thought my life was hers, forever. Now, I needed to rent a place. I knew I could afford it, so what was the problem?

The woman before me was frost dressed up. I knew about that, how people could change, but I still didn't like it, it made me nervous. I knew I'd never win her over.

'I have got savings,' I said stiffly. 'More than enough for the rent, as it happens.' I hated baring my soul like this.

'Well, that's good news,' she said, smiling. The smile went nowhere near her eyes. 'You can pay the rent for the house in advance. The whole six months.'

It was tall and rambling, in the centre of town, three storeys high, and I knew there must be something wrong, for a house this big to be offered this cheap. Well, not that cheap, but cheap enough for me to afford it. Even with all the rent in advance. I guessed it must be a wreck inside.

'How long has it been on the market?' I'd asked Gemma.

'I'm not quite sure,' said Gemma vaguely, twirling her hair around her fingers. 'About three months.'

'So why did the previous tenant leave?'

'I'm not quite sure,' she started to say, but stopped abruptly at the look on my face. 'She died, actually.'

'Ah,' I said.

'Not in the house,' said Gemma, quickly. 'She died in hospital, after a stroke. She was eighty-eight and deaf as a post, the poor old thing. She'd lived in the house all the time she was married.' She glanced ahead.

The house is a bit neglected, sadly, and I know there isn't a washing machine, but at least that means you can choose your own.'

I laughed out loud, I couldn't help it. The

woman was clearly a natural at this, she was already trained in estate agent speak. I thought she was very convincing, I guess I wanted to be convinced. The house had something, was in some ways perfect, tall and old and great for an office, as well as a home. I saw myself in my fantasy world, doing it up and making it smart, clients climbing the wide stone steps, pouring happily through the doors. Turning a shell into a home. And then I remembered.

There was no future. Not for the house, and not for me. Even now, I still forgot.

The sun went in  and all of a sudden  the day seemed  cold and the  house run down.  Gemma and I  were standing in the kitchen. I didn't like it. Gemma was right, it *was* basic.

'There *is* a fridge-freezer,' she said tersely, sensing my mood but still valiant, gesturing to an upright object, standing squat, in the middle of the room.

'What a strange place to put a fridge-freezer,' I said, indifferent.

'There's plenty of room in here,' said Gemma. 'I expect Mrs Parks thought to make it homely.'

Homely wasn't the word I'd have used. The kitchen was huge, with three old windows facing the back. They had very old glazing and strong iron bars. The glass was cracked and warped in the way that only old glass can be. Ignoring the dirt, I could barely see out. The floor was covered in cheap lino and the air of neglect was incredibly strong, I could almost smell it.

'Why don't we go upstairs,' I said.

# 2
# Then – Miranda

The pub was busy, she hated it busy, she often longed for the quiet nights when nobody came. After Da had just died. But Da had run a successful pub, the people came back, the old regulars *and* the strangers, once they knew it was alright to come. Ma didn't mind, it kept her occupied, a pity hard work wasn't enough. If only her father hadn't died.

'You mustn't say that word, Miranda,' her mother would say. 'I don't like you saying that dreadful word.'

'But he is dead, Ma,' Miranda had said, 'and he's not coming back, now, or ever. He's dead, remember?'
She shuddered to think how cruel she'd been, but at the time she couldn't have cared, she'd wanted to make her mother cry, so they could find comfort, support in each other. Instead of being split by fear and dread, of poverty, loss and not having enough.

It made Miranda feel she'd died too. And that was the worst feeling of all.

Living in Curdizan Low was hard. There were so many pubs, most of them newer or smarter than theirs. Tom once said he'd counted them all, there were over two hundred in the whole city. Miranda snapped back.

'If you've the time to count all the pubs, you're far too idle, you should be in here, helping me out. Hurry up Tom and wash these glasses.' She hadn't seen Thomas again for days.

And now, tonight, he hadn't turned up, and her ma was in another of her moods, and had gone off somewhere, not for the first time. Miranda was on her own in the bar, and people were talking about the weather, so much warmer and wasn't that good? Miranda said nothing, these people were strangers, summer in the Low was as bad as the winter, worse sometimes. There weren't any floods or the freezing nights, or having to manage on poor coal, but the smells that came with summer were worse, the dung and the flies and the local abattoirs. She swatted an imaginary fly away. Then the woman with the coat came in.

She was young and thin and Miranda's height, and wearing a hat, which made her look respectable, almost, but no decent girl would visit a pub on a Saturday night, not on her own, and Miranda knew it. The first time she'd seen her, Miranda had thought she was someone official and had called for her mother to help her out. But it turned out the woman was nobody special, for all she was pretty, and now her mother had vanished again, just like the last time. Miranda glowered.

'I'll have a jug full, love, if you would,' the young woman said, adjusting her hat and her lovely hair, tucking the thick curls under the brim.

*She doesn't deserve to have hair like that.* She poured out the ale and slopped a little.

'Your mother not in the pub tonight?'

'What's it to you?' Miranda said. She didn't see why she had to be nice. They didn't need people like her in here.

'I'm only asking, love,' said the woman. 'I thought I saw her leave just now, as I walked in. Must have been somebody else I saw.' Miranda's eyes narrowed as she watched the intruder.

'I think she's gone out looking for Thomas.' Miranda wished she hadn't spoken, she shouldn't have told the cow anything, and both of them knew the words were a lie.

'I expect you're right, my love,' said the woman.

*I'm not your love,* Miranda thought, gritting her teeth and wiping the jug. *You're hardly only a few years older than me.* She didn't know why she hated Curtis – no, she did, it was what she implied, with her looks and her manner, and the things she suggested, hinted at even. *Go why don't you, and*

43

*don't come back.*

The young woman left.

After she'd gone, Reg came up to the bar to see her. He was kind but dull and both of them knew he was sweet on her ma. He also worked part-time in the pub.

'You don't want to mix with types like her.'

'I wasn't,' said Miranda. 'I was serving her ale, like I always do.' A woman appeared, his sister Cath, she shooed Reg away and stood in his place, her eyes on Miranda.

'He's trying to tell you something, love.' Miranda waited.

'She's young, but a woman with men for friends. If you get my drift.'

Miranda nodded, she did get it. She'd known before they opened their mouths, before they started interfering. What she also got, but didn't say, was that Curtis had implied her mother was too.

# 3
# Now – Aleph

I took to the house, in a strange sort of way, it was tall and thin and elegant somehow, with a road at the front, cobbled and quaint and steps leading up to the strong front door. The rooms were vast, with very high ceilings, and although the window panes were small, and barred at the back, light came in and showed up the dust and all the potential. There was plenty of room for an office upstairs.

The third and top floor I kept for myself, including a room with huge sash windows, which gave me a view looking onto the street. Maybe the street lights would stop me from sleeping. They didn't as it happened. I was often awake.

The street was in a good part of town, although Curdizan High had once been rough. Now it was fresh with refurbished streets and tarted up buildings, apart from mine. There were plenty of tourists wandering around. I lay in my bed that very first evening, looked at the sky through curtainless windows, and heard the shouts of drunken youths. I'd never lived in the centre before, was bemused by the noise, although not that troubled. The things that kept me awake were worse. I mourned the past, and along with the past, I mourned myself, my carefree self, who'd long since died.

I must have drifted off at some point, and was woken up by children's voices. I looked at my watch, it was half past two. *Christ!* I thought, *those kids should be in bed by now.*

I dragged myself up and peered outside, but all I could see were the street lights outside, no tourists, nothing, not even an urban fox or a dog. My house was on an old cobbled road called Old School Lane, a shortcut through from Narrowboat Lane, the main shopping street. Just past my house, at the other end, the Lane curved sharply round to the left and joined a street called Scriveners Road. The kids had obviously gone that way. I swore, loudly, thinking my chance for sleep had gone. I was right, it had.

Later that day, I went to the estate agent's to return the inventory, wondering if I might see Gemma. I walked through the door and as I did, my heart sank, for there at the desk was the woman I'd met the previous time. I read the badge attached to her shirt – Marianne Parks – it made me pause. 'The previous tenant was a Mrs Parks.' She knew what I meant.

'My mother,' she said. 'She died recently. And she was the *owner*. I'll take that.'

'There's not much on it,' I told Ms Parks, talking about the inventory. 'There was too much wrong to put it all down.' Realising then, how tactless that sounded. Marianne Parks didn't bother to reply.

'How are you finding the Old Schoolhouse?' she said, slowly, for once not looking me straight in the eye.

'Is that what it was?' I said, interested. A name like that could be good for business. The woman smiled.

'Thanks for the form, Mr Jones,' she said. 'We'll send you out a copy shortly.' She turned away, I was being dismissed. I headed for the door, thinking; I decided to pay a visit to the library. As yet no clients had found me in Curdizan.

'Have you heard them yet, Mr Jones?' she said. I stopped, short.

'What did you say?' I said sharply, turning around.

'Have you heard the children's voices in the night?'

'Yes,' I said. 'I heard them last night, about half past two. Parents these days are far too lax.'

'And were the children crying or laughing?'

'Neither,' I said. 'They were chattering loudly,

in high pitched voices. I was half asleep when they woke me up. Tourists, I guess.'

Marianne Parks gave a slow, small smile, a smile that made me feel quite uneasy. But not as much as the words that followed.

'No, Mr Jones, they weren't tourists, or even the kids who live around here. The children you heard were the School Lane ghosts.'

# 4
# Then – Thomas

I should have been helping Miranda in the pub, but instead I went up to Curdizan High, to look for Louise. The High's the part where the abbey is, as well as my school, although nothing about the place is high. I walked past the school and finally came to Pearson's Tenements, that's where she lives, but Louise wasn't there, surprise, surprise. I wasn't surprised, the place was a dump, but all the same, I had to look. The tenement building was tall and grim, tiny spaces joined by a stairway and open landings, the black of the open night in between. I thought they were more like rooms than landings, people's possessions scattered about, rooms on the outside. I thought of escape.

I once saw a woman jump from a landing, far too high from the ground to be safe, but almost worse, too low to be dead, and gone in a flash. They patched her up, as best as they could, and she even went back to her room for a bit, but she never walked the same after that and not long after, finally died. I didn't know it at the time, but her name was May, and she was also Louise's ma. I never did learn which room she came from.

It's a maze inside the tenement building, stair after stair to each new landing, the landings themselves being almost homes, with chairs or a table and a dog chained up and even the odd bit of carpet or rug. But the landings were cold, an outside cold and all exposed to kids like me.

I shivered, scared in the black of the stairway, I knew I ought to go back, and soon. Miranda would be wondering where I was. But I'd promised old Pike I'd find Louise.

'He's *Mister* Pike,' my ma would say, but she didn't know Pike the way I knew him, he didn't deserve to be called *Mister*. He was cold, indifferent and sometimes cruel; he'd said if I didn't find Louise, he'd throw her out of the school for good, and she'd end up lost, like Miranda's ma. I didn't know what he meant by that, but I didn't much like the way he'd said it, and I liked Louise, she wasn't rough like most of the kids, and she lived in a flea pit, storeys high. If I had to live in Pearson's Tenements, in amongst all the privy smells, I'm sure I'd forget to go to school. School would be just a dream or something.

I reached a landing, the fourth or fifth, I didn't know which, so I tossed a huge stone over the edge, and counted until I heard it land. Although I'd looked, I hadn't found her. I'd even tried a few of the doors, but nobody seemed to know her name. A shadow slunk by and I held my breath, you're never alone in a place like this. I turned around, got ready to run, but a hand shot out and grabbed my collar, pulling me back, very sharply. Somebody's hand against my mouth. The somebody spoke.

'Tom, Thomas, you shouldn't be here, I haven't the time to look for you. I wouldn't have come, and won't the next time, it's only because your ma was worried.'

*Ma, worried?* That was a laugh. I snorted, loudly, and wriggled my collar out of her grasp. It was Miranda from the pub, looking wild as always, her eyes glowing bright in the light from the moon. She tossed her hair and I stared right back.

'How did you know I was here?' I said.

'I know you well enough by now. The sort of place you like to go. Each to their own, that's what I say.'

She looked around as we walked back down and hurried along the shabby street, all shadows and shade and stinking gutters. A rat rushed past and Miranda's nose twitched, as if to say, *You see what I mean?* I grinned in the dark, I liked rats and I liked Miranda, although not as much as I liked Louise.

'I presume you're coming back with me?' Miranda asked, as we stopped on the corner by

Curdizan Church, the church that stood in the shade of the abbey. I nodded, sadly.

'Yes,' I said, torn between my longing for a pie at the end of my shift, and the word I'd given to find Louise. Shame on me, for the hot pie won. We hurried down Scriveners Road to the alley, through the alley to Convent Court and down to the streets called Curdizan Low.

'Don't be dragging your heels,' said Miranda. 'I'm supposed to be serving ale right now, and washing the glasses you didn't do.'

I smiled to myself as we hurried along. Collecting the glasses and washing them after was what I was paid for, and I liked my job at the Keepsake Arms. The money I earned from my job at the pub helped my ma, and it helped Miranda, her da was dead and Mrs Collenge was never around.

Miranda was good in the pub, I thought, cheerful and bright, but not too friendly, sharp enough to keep them drinking, spending their money, not talking to her. I wished again, like I'd wished before, that she was my sister and not just a girl who could boss me around. Neighbours and mates, that's what we were, even though she was all grown up. Miranda Collenge was eighteen.

# 5
# Now – Aleph

Marianne Parks' words shocked me. *I've never believed in ghosts*, I thought, *so why start now?* Or at least, not the ones that weren't in my head. I cycled home in the fading light, forgetting my plan to go to the library, hardly aware of the world around me. Something had shifted inside my head. Starting again was proving to be what I'd guessed all along, another illusion. *You're never allowed to forget*, I thought.

I'd wanted to ask Ms Parks some more but she didn't seem eager to talk fully. The door had opened and someone walked in, another gullible tenant, probably, eager to part with some hard-earned cash. I left them alone.

I cycled away, vaguely troubled, and now with even more questions than answers. I rode with care down Narrowboat Lane, ducking my head when I came to the arch. I was almost home when a woman stepped out in front of the bike. I braked, sharply. The woman shrieked and her shopping and handbag fell to the ground.

Old School Lane was pedestrianised, which was just as well in the present circumstances. I dropped my bike and hurried towards her. The woman was struggling to pick up her parcels, margarine, bread and a bag of potatoes, all in one hand. Her other hand was glued to her ankle. *At least she's alive*, I thought, detached. My mind froze over.

'Are you alright?' I heard myself say.

'I think I've sprained my ankle,' she said.

When she finally removed her fingers, it was true the ankle seemed slightly puffy, a reddish colour, rather than pale. I picked up her handbag and gathered her food. 'My house is just here,' I told the stranger. 'Please come inside, I'll bandage that up.'

'Oh no, it's okay,' the woman replied, but her voice was faint and the no meant yes. I helped her make her way up the steps. Once inside, I steered her gently into the kitchen, and then to a chair, putting her shopping by her side.

'Would you like tea, or maybe some whisky?' I paused, waiting.

'Whisky, please,' she said smiling, her eyes darting all over the place. 'This is quite some kitchen, much bigger than mine. You've got so much space.'

'It's certainly different,' I said, dryly, passing her a mug with the whisky in it. 'I've just moved in so there aren't any glasses.' I sat down opposite the stranger and smiled.

'Aleph Jones? That's your name?' The woman was reading the estate agent's brochure; I'd put it there beside my tea.

'Yes, that's right. I know it's unusual, everybody says so.'

'A name to go with the house, I'd say. Quite unique.' She took a deep breath and looked behind her, stared at the hall. 'I'd love to have a look at the place; does that sound rude?'

*A little bit forward, perhaps,* I thought, but I wasn't offended, not in the least. Then she blushed.

'Not now, of course, not with the ankle. Climbing the stairs might be too much.'

'I'd offer to run you home,' I said. 'But I don't have a car.' I stopped abruptly. The woman smiled.

'I don't suppose you need one here, in the centre of town? Isn't this road pedestrianised?'

'Yes,' I said. 'But not round the corner in Scriveners Road. Would you like me to call a taxi?'

'When you're ready,' she said, lightly, and I realised then how lovely she was. Her hair was short and slightly spiky, her dark eyes chocolate, the Bournville kind. She was casually dressed, but quite impressive. I stood up abruptly.

'I'll do it now,' I said and vanished, and before very long the taxi was booked.

The rest of our time together passed quickly. She said she'd come into town to shop, I told her

I'd meant to go to the library. I didn't say why.

The taxi turned up before I was ready and I noticed her looking around at the hall. I was suddenly seized by a crazy moment, the sort that defines one's life forever, and I asked this woman, who I'd only just met, to come back again and eat with me. 'Tomorrow?' I said.

'I can't tomorrow,' she said, softly. 'I'm going away for a few days' break. With Alice, my daughter.'

She watched my face as she said the word *daughter*, and it felt to me like some sort of test.

'Well how about a week tomorrow?'

We agreed on that and parted happily; she managed the steps to the street quite well. When I'd finally closed the door on my guest, my mind began to drift in reverse, recalling my chat with Marianne Parks.

'You asked if the children were laughing or crying, the School Lane ghosts. Why did you ask that?'

'It's just a rumour, Mr Jones.'

'Yes, Ms Parks, but what rumour?'

'They say it depends on who you are. The good hear laughter, the bad, crying, or even screaming. It's all rubbish, Mr Jones.' She sniffed loudly.

'My mother lived there most of her life, after she married, and she never heard the ghosts, not once.'

*But wasn't your mother deaf?* I thought.

Those were the thoughts that engaged my mind as I cycled back to the Old Schoolhouse, and caused me to fail to see Cressida Sewell. As time went on I recalled those words again and again, with good reason. I often heard the children at night, just around midnight and sometimes later. But from that day on, they were always sad.

# 6
# Then – Thomas

*Mister* Pike was the same as always, bored and boring. I didn't know why he turned up at all, I thought it was kids who were meant to hate school. I did, often. But I also liked the porridge they gave us.

I shifted my bum on the hard wooden seat and played around with a couple of words. The work we did was far too easy, my ma had taught me to read already. I was proud of being able to read and write, most of the lads I knew couldn't count, let alone read. I wanted a better paid job than my da, he worked at the mill, when he was sober. A lot of the time he just didn't turn up.

The mill was everything in our street. We were right at the bottom on Haversham Road, our house backed onto the factory walls, you could the hear the generator's constant hum. Because our house backed onto the factory, it was dark at the back, there weren't any windows. There wasn't much light at the front either, the factory's silos towered above us and blocked off most of the sky and sun. Not far away was the factory chimney, belching out horrible smells all day. I hated our street.

I felt the sting as a huge piece of chalk bounced off my arm and onto the floor and under my chair. I seriously thought about throwing it back.

'Time to quit dreaming and starting working, Islip, unless you'd like to be out on your ear.' Pike was yelling as loud as ever but somehow it never made any difference.

'Plenty of lads would like to be you, sitting in the warm and dry all day. Lads who act a little bit grateful, not as if they can't be bothered.'

*Warm? In here?* He'd got to be joking. I glanced at my feet, which were bare as usual. Ma said I couldn't wear shoes in summer, or even in spring, the money for shoes just didn't exist. Despite all three of us having a job.

I felt a tiny twinge of guilt. Because I'd been late to the pub last night, I'd be docked some pay and Ma would be short, she was always short. My father drank it all away. She wouldn't be pleased that I'd turned up late and she'd no doubt give me some stick for that. But at least I had a ma to go home to, unlike Louise, whose mother was dead. I tried not to think of Louise anymore. Even more guilt.

It wasn't because Louise was missing, I'd done my best, I'd tried to find her, Louise was a mate, she loved to climb trees and beat me at conkers, and when it was hot we swam in the Blue. Our house and the factory were both by the river, which wasn't as good as you'd think it would be. Not when the days were really warm and the dung had been dumped by the corporation.

No, I felt guilty for something else. I hadn't gone looking for Louise at all, despite what I'd said to Miranda later. Looking for her was what I'd done after, after I'd given up looking for Alice. Alice was totally different to Louise; *she* was a girl, all flowers and hair, and pretty to boot. Strangely enough, that's why I liked her.

I was walking home from school one day, just pottering really, kicking at stones and picking up wood we'd use for the fire, and then in the distance, I saw Alice.

She was right by the gate that led to the church on Scriveners Road, Curdizan Church, and holding something in her hand. It was big and square and flashed in the light. She saw me looking, and put it away in her bag, quickly. *Posh*, I thought, and I couldn't resist walking closer. Her bag was blue and it looked so clean, as if it was new, and her blonde hair shone and wasn't tied back, *and* she wore shoes, all glossy and smart. None of the kids I knew wore shoes. *Slumming it,* I thought and scowled, jealous, and strangely angry, bitter and resentful. I wanted to live like them, I did, nobody wants to live in a dump. *Sorry Ma.*

I thought the girl would run away, she was far too smart, and I looked a scruff, with my shirt hanging out and my trousers baggy, and me being the third person to have them, but she didn't run away, she just stood there, staring, so I walked closer.

'I'm called Tom. Who are you?'

The girl didn't answer, just shook her head, so I tried again, a different tack.

'Do you live around here? That's my school, across the graveyard.' I pointed behind us. 'That's the door to the joinery workshop, some of the lads are training in woodwork.'

I thought she'd ask if I was one of the lads in training, but she still didn't speak, so I prattled on.

'There are also some lads who are going to be stonemasons, working on the church.'

I saw her glance across at the church and I laughed out loud and shook my head. 'Not *Curdizan Church,* the proper church, the abbey up there.' The abbey twinkled in the sun. She still didn't answer. I felt uneasy.

'Cat got your tongue?' I said impatient.

She shook her head, then pointed to herself and clamped her teeth shut. *Then* I got it.

'You're dumb,' I said. 'You can't speak.'

She hesitated slightly, then she nodded.

'Alright,' I said. 'I can write, can you?' She laughed at that and her blue eyes sparkled, as bright as the sky. *Of course she can write, you stupid prat. She's posh, and rich.*

'I don't have anything to write on,' I said. I felt helpless, useless somehow. Her smile widened.

*But I do*, she said, and although she hadn't opened her mouth, I could hear her voice as clear as a bell. It was light and fine and sounded like summer. And then she brought the thing from her bag.

**Thank you for reading this extract** from *Shadows of the Lost Child*. If you'd like to find out what happens to Alice and Tom, you can find the book on Amazon at:

**http://tinyurl.com/nbofbnv** (UK)

**http://tinyurl.com/ks3ksng** (US)

The novel is available both in print and as an ebook.

## Some Amazon Reviews

'Really enjoyed this atmospheric story. Plot kept me hooked with its mystery, ghosts and time travel. Lots of things going on to keep you interested.' (Jilly)

'A fascinating book taking the reader seamlessly from past to present and back again in what seems like a parallel universe. Clever, detailed and very imaginative.' J Foden

# G. Watching Charlotte Brontë Die: and other surreal stories
(Extract from title story)

by **Ellie Stevenson**

Rosegate Publications, 2013
ISBN: 978-0-9572165-2-5

## The Extract

We'd been in the flat a year when it happened.

The night had been cold, and extremely wet. I was sitting in my chair, over by the window.

My wife was out working, she usually was. It was then that I heard it, an enormous crash, a screech and a thud, followed by silence. Someone's life, played out on the pavement. It wasn't the first time our street had done that, claimed a victim, with its deadly camber, its rain-stroked curve. The road was treacherous, sometimes lethal.

I leapt from my chair and ran to the window. She was lying there, in the middle of the tarmac, broken, damaged, her head to one side. She was calm and quiet and didn't move, and the bike beside her was bent out of shape. My heart stopped beating. It was Charlotte Brontë.

And it looked to me as if she was dead.

I dressed quickly, with trembling fingers, opened the door and ran down the stairs. The street would be empty, it was access only, apart from the tourists. There were no tourists on the street that night. I opened the door that led to outside and looked to the right, she'd be just around the bend. I rounded it quickly, as fast as I could. There was nobody there.

I blinked sharply and looked again, in case I'd missed her. I saw the rain, it was heavier now, streaming down gutters, flooding the road. I saw the light on an empty can, a broken bottle, remains of a toy. But that was all. No bike wheels spinning high in the air, no ghastly corpse, or crumpled victim propped against a wall. The street was damp and devoid of life, but also of death. I watched the water running away. All I could think was one small thought. I hadn't known Charlotte could ride a bike.

It wasn't the first time I'd seen her.

My wife has a job at the local uni, teaching English, she loves all things Brontë. That's how we met, at a Brontë conference, in West Yorkshire. I married my wife because I love her, but also because she looks like Charlotte. I should feel guilty, but I don't, not at all. I'm privately pleased and secretly proud, as if I've discovered a hidden treasure. Perhaps I have.

Charlotte Brontë, born again.

My skills and training are different from my wife's. *I'm* not a teacher, I'm a writer's researcher, but that's ok, I love my work. I study theology as well as the Brontës, ferret out the facts from the archives. And I love the place where I find those facts, a cathedral library, and that's the place where I first saw Charlotte. Not in one of the first editions, but there in person, right by the shelves.

I was up in the gallery, quietly working. Dozens of volumes piled up high. They were all so beautiful, all so original, it's a wonder I did any work at all. I was taking a tract from the nearest shelf when I heard a noise and looked right down to the room below and there she was, right beneath me, and all lit up from the stained glass windows. I caught my breath. She was just like the photos, quaint and homely with a small, shy smile and rosebud lips. But her eyes were different, cool, piercing and quite unlike the rest of her look. Even though we were far apart, and I was standing up in the gallery, I could see those eyes, see them stare through me. I watched and waited, noticed her beckon. But she still didn't speak.

Forgetting where I was, I walked over to the railing. I forgot that the railing, normally solid and made of cast iron, had been replaced by a tape for repairs. Nobody ever came up here. All there was between me and a fall, a terrible drop, maybe death, was a thin strip of tape, not even taut. I was seconds away from the worst that could happen. I stopped suddenly, looked down at the floor. Miss Brontë had gone. I was safe, for the moment.

But she always came back.

**Thank you for reading this extract from** *Watching Charlotte* Brontë *Die: and other surreal stories.* If you'd like to find out what happens next, or read the other scary stories, you can find the collection on Amazon at:

**http://amzn.to/19dCdEY** (UK)

**http://amzn.to/1Cobsq7** (US)

The novel is available both in print and as an ebook.

## Some Amazon Reviews

'Entertaining book of short stories. Pleased with my purchase. Highly recommended.' (Jilly)

'This collection of stories is both entertaining but with a surreal twist. I enjoyed all of them immensely... would recommend.' (Lundylupin)

# H. Ship of Haunts:
## the other Titanic story
(Extract from the novel)

### by Ellie Stevenson

Rosegate Publications, 2012
ISBN: 978-0-9572165-01

### About Ship of Haunts

Carrin remembers a past life – on Titanic. And now she's being stalked by a ghost from the ship.

Lily the ghost is searching for her cousin. She's crossed time to find Lucie, but now time is running out.

One hundred years after the ship sank, Carrin's shipmates are gathered together to remember Titanic. But who can she trust – certainly not the man who drowned her. But can she even trust herself?

For Carrin has a terrible secret, one she's been

hiding all her life. But at least Lily's on her side. Or so she thinks.

From the heat of the harsh Australian sun to the darkest depths of the ocean floor, Ship of Haunts is a novel of conflicts.

Carrin is scared and Lily is desperate, both of them in a race against time. Will they manage to make it through, including surviving the vengeful Mad?

# 1
# Carrin's Story – 2012

Not every girl gets stalked by a ghost. Or haunted by a ship.

The ghost was called Lily but the ship came first. It always did. The ship was Titanic. I drowned on that ship.

I was up on the deck, right at the top, running and running, as fast as I could, towards the stern. Away from the water, around my feet. I wasn't alone.

And though I ran fast, as fast as I could, the stern rose up, out of the water, and we rose with it, slipping and sliding on a frigid deck. Not everyone made it.

I grabbed for a railing and held on tight, feeling the steel dig into my skin. I knew it was hopeless. Many more people did just the same. And then the stern shifted, twisted and turned, a corkscrew ride, high in the air. We held our place, just for a second. Then down she fell, faster and faster, heading for the bottom, where no-one ever goes. And then I fell off.

My arms flailed and I let out a scream, one more voice, in amongst the rest.

'I'm going to die. I'm going to die.'

And die is exactly what I did.

But unlike the others, I had help.

I said there was a ghost and her name was Lily. Not that I knew she was called Lily to begin with, she was just a voice, driving me crazy.

I first met Lily in 1912, when I lived before. Now you know it. I *am* crazy.

Well maybe you're right, but why don't you ask me where we met?

We met on Titanic, which sank in the night on her maiden voyage, in 1912.

Such a beautiful ship, sailing the ocean, and then – nothing.

So many died – fifteen hundred people, it was tragedy, failure, on dozens of counts.

And the last sentence, very important.

I was there.

# 2
# Lily's Story – 1911

I was proud to be called a Yorkshire girl, Yorkshire had made me what I was. I never wanted to leave the north. But since I had...

When Mother gave me the crumpled letter I knew it was bad. Give it to Maddy, is what she said. Maddy will help. I didn't care. I knew it was bad, without the letter, her white, pinched face and the constant cough. I opened the letter. Just as I thought.

Lucie and I had to go south. To a place called Southampton.

Three days later, my sister emerged from Mother's bedroom. Her face was pale, as pale as a ghost. 'Mother's gone,' she said to me sadly. 'What will we do?'

I pulled the letter out of my pocket. 'We're off to Southampton, to stay with our aunt, Madeleine Rawlins. Mother arranged it.' Lucie blinked.

Lucie was distant, dark and plump, not a bit like me, although we were sisters. I was tall and fair, with thin skinny bones and flyaway hair. Lucie was pretty, I had to protect her. I thought Southampton would keep us safe, would keep the wolf away from the door. How wrong can you be?

Aunt Maddy's house was a total shock. We'd lived in a farmhouse, out in the fields, in a place called Linsit. Linsit was vast, with moors and the cliffs, and the Bay below us, with us in between. We were renting a farm and managing somehow, then Mother died. Aunt Maddy's house was completely different, right in the town, it was tall and thin, just like her. She didn't seem all that pleased to see us.

'So you're Lucie?' she said to my sister, her cold eyes sharp.

Lucie just stood there, silent, as always. Maddy was dark, like Lucie was dark, but Madeleine Rawlins' face was cold. She was watchful and wary and didn't look like my mother at all. I didn't warm to this woman one bit. But I had to try.

'Good to meet you at last, Aunt Maddy,' I said to her, taking her hand. She didn't bother to look my way.

'I'm not your aunt,' she insisted sharply, looking at Lucie. 'I'm far too young to be anyone's aunt.' It was true she was, being barely thirty, and now expecting a child of her own. But she *was* my aunt, my mother's sister. I also thought she was Lucie's aunt. My mistake.

Her man, Joss Rawlins, who she called her husband, when he wasn't, had just got a job. He was a stoker by trade, he worked on the ships, shovelling coal. Or at least, he had, until the coal strike started. No-one had worked on the ships in months, because of the strike. For a place like Southampton, which lived by its docks, the strike was bad news. And it made Joss restless, hungry for change.

I knew how he felt, I was restless too, I wanted a life, a world full of colour, not grey, grimy streets and second-hand clothes. I had my adventures, stealing mostly, we needed the food, that was my excuse. The truth was, I loved the excitement. I also stole things I could pawn later.

But a new dawn was coming, a ship called Titanic, and Joss signed up, Aunt Maddy couldn't stop him. I could see it in his eyes, he was eager to leave, his woman expecting and two teenage girls who weren't his own. It was then I had my fatal idea.

I thought it would give us, Lucie and me, a much better future. I also thought it would free up Mad.

That was my third and final mistake.

**Thank you for reading this extract** from *Ship of Haunts: the other Titanic Story.* If you'd like to find out what happens to Carrin and Lily on Titanic, you can find the book on Amazon at:

**http://amzn.to/1FeR2Ts** (UK)

**http://amzn.to/1GJm3AS** (US)

The novel is available both in print and as an ebook.

# Some Amazon Reviews

'Even those who don't really go for ghosts and the supernatural will enjoy this book because the characters are so captivating, and the historical events are well described and conform to what we know from history, i.e. the author has done her research and it shows. A thoroughly enjoyable book!' V Salvemini

'From the beginning I was drawn into the lives of the numerous characters in the novel and was gripped by the detailed descriptions of historical events/settings, in particular, life on Titanic and life as a child migrant in Australia during 1940s. It is clear that the author has researched the factual information thoroughly and the settings and events feel very real.' S Davies

# I. About the Author

Ellie Stevenson has written two novels, *Shadows of the Lost Child* (Rosegate Publications, 2014; Amazon: B00NGSSVM2) and *Ship of Haunts: the other Titanic story* (Rosegate Publications, 2012; Amazon: B007SPGR98), both partly historical mysteries with a dash of the mystical and some ghosts.

*Shadows of the Lost Child* was inspired by historic York (UK).

Ellie has also written *Watching Charlotte Brontë Die: and other surreal stories* (Rosegate Publications, 2013; Amazon: B00AZYXASU).  Her writing is fuelled by inspiration, determination and plenty of coffee.

**Find her on:**

**Facebook:**
http://www.facebook.com/Stevensonauthor

**Twitter:**
http://twitter.com/Stevensonauthor

**Pinterest:**
http://uk.pinterest.com/stevensonauthor

**Blog:**
http://elliestevenson.wordpress.com (the Haunted Historian: haunting the page across time)

Thanks for reading!

If you have found *Writing for Magazines in the UK* useful, please leave a review on Amazon. Thank you.

Lightning Source UK Ltd.
Milton Keynes UK
UKOW04f1148280815

257694UK00002B/9/P